CONTENTS

The Viking Age 4
Learning more from archaeology.......................................7

Viking Society 8
The Oseberg ship burial..8
Rich and poor..10
How society was governed 12
Discovering Thingvellir 12
Law, crime and punishment..14
Religion 15

Daily Life 16
Discovering Brattahlid..16
Food and farming...18

Trade and Towns 20
Discovering Birka...20
Town life 22

Vikings at War 24
Discovering Repton..24
Warriors and weapons...26

Ships and Seafaring 28
Discovering Roskilde..29
Shipbuilding and navigation 30
Vikings around the world 32
Discovering L'Anse-aux-Meadows......................................33

Art, Learning and Religion 34
Discovering Gotland...34
Gods and goddesses 36
The arrival of Christianity 38
Discovering Jelling 39
Runes and writing..40

Archaeology Today 42

Timeline of the Viking Age 44
Timeline of Viking Archaeology.......................................45
Glossary 46
Index 48

Dates BC and AD

BC after a date means before the birth of Christ. The years count down to 0, the date that has been taken as the year when Jesus Christ was born.

AD before a date stands for the Latin *anno domini* ('the year of the lord'). It means that the date is counted from after Christ's birth in the year 0.

Any words appearing in the text in bold, **like this**, are explained in the Glossary.

THE VIKING AGE

The people known as the Vikings came from three countries in north-west Europe – Denmark, Norway and Sweden – and the period known as the Viking Age began when some of them left their homelands in the late 8th century AD. For about 300 years, Vikings **raided**, explored and traded with many countries. They also founded many settlements, some of which continued to exist long after the Viking Age was over.

▽ Viking settlements often grew up on coasts and riverbanks, as they were the first places that the invaders reached in their powerful ships. Some settlements were also founded on fertile farmland, while others developed from existing towns.

A changing world

In the 8th century, most people from Scandinavia (the area of Europe containing Denmark, Norway and Sweden) were farmers. Then important changes began to affect this way of life. It was probably these changes

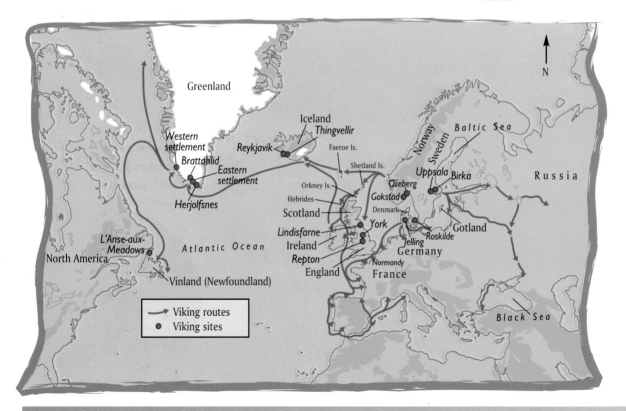

EXCAVATING THE PAST

THE VIKING WORLD

Christine Hatt

Heinemann
LIBRARY

www.heinemann.co.uk/library
Visit our website to find out more information about **Heinemann Library** books.

To order:
☎ Phone 44 (0) 1865 888066
🖹 Send a fax to 44 (0) 1865 314091
💻 Visit the Heinemann Bookshop at www.heinemann.co.uk/library to browse our catalogue and order online.

First published in Great Britain by Heinemann Library, Halley Court, Jordan Hill, Oxford OX2 8EJ, part of Harcourt Education.

Heinemann is a registered trademark of Harcourt Education Ltd.

© Harcourt Education Ltd 2004
First published in paperback in 2005
The moral right of the proprietor has been asserted.

Editorial: Nicole Irving, Kate Bellamy and Ruth Nason
Design: Carol Binding
Picture Research: Shelley Noronha
Production: Edward Moore

Originated by Ambassador Litho Ltd
Printed in China by WKT

ISBN 0 431 14240 8 (hardback)
08 07 06 05 04
10 9 8 7 6 5 4 3 2 1

ISBN 0 431 14247 5 (paperback)
09 08 07 06 05
10 9 8 7 6 5 4 3 2 1

British Library Cataloguing in Publication Data
Christine Hatt
The Viking World – (Excavating the Past)
948'.022

A full catalogue record for this book is available from the British Library.

Acknowledgements
The publishers would like to thank the following for permission to reproduce photographs: Alamy: p. **14**; The Art Archive: pp. **30, 34, 35** bottom, **36** top, **36** bottom, **40, 41;** BBC Photo Archives: p. **26** top; Dan Carlsson, Gotland University: p. **43;** Corbis: p. **22** (Ted Spiegel), **39** (Carmen Redondo); Malcolm Gibb: p. **31** top; Topham/Polfoto: pp. **38, 42;** University Museum of Cultural Heritage, University of Oslo, Norway: pp. **9** top (O. Vaering), **16** (Ove Holst); The Viking Ship Museum, Denmark: p. **29** (Werner Karrasch); Werner Forman Archive: pp. **5** (Statens Historiska Museum, Stockholm), **6** (Universitetetsbiblioteket, Uppsala, Sweden), **7** (Viking Ship Museum, Bygdoy), **9** bottom (Viking Ship Museum, Bygdoy), **10** (Viking Ship Museum, Bygdoy), **11** (Viking Ship Museum, Bygdoy), **12, 15** top (Statens Historiska Museum, Stockholm), **17, 18** (Thjodminjasafn, Reykjavik, Iceland [National Museum]), **20** (Statens Historiska Museum, Stockholm), **23** top (Statens Historiska Museum, Stockholm), **23** bottom (Statens Historiska Museum, Stockholm), **26** bottom (Liverpool City Museum, Liverpool), **27** (Upplsndsmuseet, Uppsala), **28** top, **28** bottom (Viking Ship Museum, Bygdoy), **31** bottom (Viking Ship Museum, Bygdoy), **35, 37** (Thjodminjasafn, Reykjavik, Iceland [National Museum]); York Archaeological Trust: pp. **15** bottom, **19, 21, 25, 32.**

Cover photograph of a Viking house in Jarlshof, Shetland, reproduced with permission of Corbis. The small photograph of a Viking nobleman's necklace reproduced with permission of Werner Forman.

The publishers would like to thank Dr Ailsa Mainman, Assistant Director, York Archaeological Trust, for her assistance in the preparation of this book.

Every effort has been made to contact copyright holders of any material reproduced in this book. Any omissions will be rectified in subsequent printings if notice is given to the publishers.

that led men to sail away in search of wealth and adventure. Scandinavians called this activity going 'a-viking', from which the name 'Viking' probably comes.

One of the changes was population growth. As the number of people increased, it became more difficult to find good land to farm, and so people started to look elsewhere. Another change was increased contact with other parts of Europe, where strong new countries were growing up. Sometimes this contact took the form of trade, and important trading towns grew up. Sometimes the Vikings seized opportunities to attack and rob rich settlements and monasteries.

A third change was growing violence between men who were fighting for power in Scandinavia. Some were probably forced out of their homelands by rivals, while some chose to leave so that they could go raiding and then use their **loot** to pay their supporters. Others may have decided that they could not win at home, so would set up new settlements abroad.

Ship-building skills

The Vikings could travel long distances because they were expert ship-builders. As well as narrow wooden **longships**, for sailing to war, they built wider ships for taking people and their possessions to establish settlements, and strong vessels called **knorrs** for carrying trade cargoes. All Viking ships had both sails and oars.

Many people think that Viking warriors wore helmets with two horns sticking out of the top. In fact, during all their excavations, **archaeologists** have found no examples of horned helmets. The idea that Vikings wore them probably grew up during the 19th century, when artists first drew them in that way.

△ ▽ *Archaeologists found these coins depicting Viking longships in the Viking marketplace at Birka, Sweden.*

Expansion and settlement

The first known Viking raid took place in 793, when Norwegians attacked a **monastery** on the English island of Lindisfarne. For the next 50 years, Norwegian and Danish Vikings continued to steal goods and terrorize people, not only in England, but also in other European lands. Then, from the mid-9th century, their tactics changed and they began to found settlements, eventually even reaching North America. Meanwhile Swedish Vikings, known as Rus, travelled eastwards and eventually gave their name to a new state – Russia.

As Vikings travelled the world, major changes continued to take place at home. Gradually, the fights between rival leaders ended and Scandinavia **converted** from **paganism** to Christianity. By the 11th century in Denmark and Norway, and by the 12th century in Sweden, kings and queens were in control of united countries and daily life had become more stable. The Viking Age was over.

EYEWITNESS

'And they came to the church of Lindisfarne, laid everything waste [destroyed everything] …, trampled the holy places with polluted feet, dug up the altars and seized all the treasures …'

(An 8th-century account of the Viking raid on Lindisfarne, by Simeon of Durham)

▽ *Snorri Sturluson's book retelling the Viking myths is known as the 'Prose Edda'.*

WHO WAS Snorri Sturluson?

*Snorri Sturluson was a Christian writer in Iceland in the 13th century. He was interested in the Vikings who had settled in his homeland in about 870, so he learned all that he could about them. Later he wrote books known as **sagas** about what he had discovered. One book retold **myths** about the Viking gods. Another was a history of the kings of Norway. Experts think that the books are great literature, but they do not think that they are always completely reliable guides to the past, because they were written so long after the Viking Age.*

Learning more from archaeology

Historians can discover some facts about the Viking Age by reading documents from the time. However, few documents remain, and they are often unreliable. To learn more, experts turn to archaeology, the study of the past through the examination of old objects and **ruins**. Archaeologists, many from universities and museums in Scandinavia, have been **excavating** Viking sites since the 19th century. In the early days especially, many were driven by a new pride in Scandinavian history, and a wish to show that there was more to Viking culture than violence.

▷ *Among the most spectacular Viking discoveries made by archaeologists was a burial site at Oseberg in Norway. This carving of a Viking face is from a beautiful wooden cart found at the site.*

In this book you will find out about some of the most spectactular Viking discoveries made by archaeologists. You will also see how the sites and **artefacts** have provided experts with more information about the Viking way of life. In the 21st century, excavations are continuing in many places. Although much has already been discovered, there is still more to learn about the daring raiders, traders and settlers who left their Scandinavian homelands many hundreds of years ago.

Archaeology Challenge

Archaeologists are always looking for new techniques to help them. For example, many are now turning to the science of genetics, the study of how characteristics of living things pass from generation to generation. Genetic information is stored in DNA, a substance in human **cells**. By comparing the DNA of modern humans in the Viking homelands with the DNA of modern humans in places where the Vikings settled, scientists hope to discover which people around the world are descended from Scandinavians.

Viking society was made up of three groups: kings, queens and **nobles** at the top, **freemen** in the middle and slaves at the bottom. Royal people and nobles were usually rich and powerful, while the wealth of freemen depended on how much land they owned. There were several types of slave. Experts think that some Vikings were born into slavery, some became temporary slaves while they were in debt and others became slaves after they were captured during **raids** overseas.

The Oseberg ship burial

Vikings sometimes buried their dead in ships, then built an earth mound on top. This may have been because they believed that, after death, people had to travel to a new world. With the body, people usually buried possessions that they thought the dead person would need. The quality of these **grave goods** often showed how important a person was in Viking society.

In 1904 **archaeologists**, led by Professor Gabriel Gustafsson, **excavated** a fine ship burial in Oseberg, Norway. They discovered not only a magnificently carved wooden ship from the 9th century, but an exceptional collection of grave goods. These included a four-wheeled cart, four **sledges**, five beds and some faded **tapestries** made of silk and wool. There were also everyday items, such as spades and sewing equipment. Experts think that there had once been costly jewellery in the ship, too, but it had been stolen by grave-robbers.

Archaeology Challenge

The skeletons at Oseberg were buried in a wooden chamber. As the chamber was made of oak, archaeologists were able to use a technique called tree-ring dating to find out the age of the wood. The technique works because tree trunks grow a new ring of wood around their centres every year. Each ring is different, as each year has different weather conditions. So by looking at the ring pattern, experts can tell how old wood is. At Oseberg, they found that the burial chamber oaks had been cut down in 834.

WHO WAS Gabriel Gustafsson?

Gabriel Gustafsson was a Swedish professor, who at the time of the Oseberg excavation was director of the University Museum in Oslo, Norway. He did not discover the ship burial mound, but learned about it from a local farmer, who brought some pieces of wood from the site to show him. Gustafsson instantly recognized the importance of the find and never forgot the date in August 1903 when he learned about it. It was his 50th birthday!

Royal remains?

Archaeologists also discovered two skeletons in the grave. One belonged to a woman of about 50, the other to a woman between 20 and 30. As the grave goods were so luxurious, experts believe that one of the women was a queen or noblewoman. They also think that the other woman may have been a slave. In Viking times, slaves were sometimes killed and then buried alongside the dead person whom they had served in life.

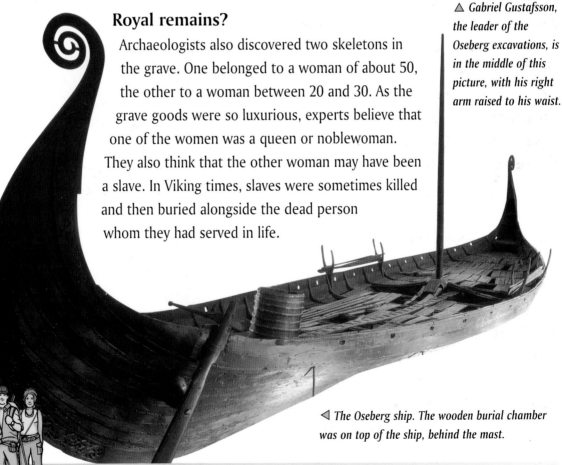

△ Gabriel Gustafsson, the leader of the Oseberg excavations, is in the middle of this picture, with his right arm raised to his waist.

◁ The Oseberg ship. The wooden burial chamber was on top of the ship, behind the mast.

Rich and poor

Information from the grave

Archaeologists are not sure which of the Oseberg skeletons was the queen and which the slave, but the fact that grave-robbers had cut off the right hand and left upper arm of the older woman provided a clue. The thieves probably removed these body parts to steal the jewellery on them, so it is likely that the woman was wearing precious rings and bracelets. This suggests, but does not prove, that she was of noble birth.

Experts have been able to find out much more about rich Vikings by examining the Oseberg grave goods. This and other graves discovered across the Viking world have also taught them a little about slaves.

EYEWITNESS

'When a chief has died his family ask his slave women and slaves, "Who will die with him?" Then one of them says "I will." When she has said this there is no backing out...'

(A 10th-century account by Arab trader Ibn Fadlan of a Viking funeral in Russia.)

A cart – and horses

This four-wheeled cart found at Oseberg was probably designed to carry the dead to their home in the afterlife. It was not an everyday vehicle – its sides were covered in elaborate carvings of people, snakes and other animals. The quality of the carvings suggests that they were made in a royal workshop, so also shows the high rank and wealth of at least one of the grave's inhabitants.

The people who arranged the Oseberg burial did not forget that the cart and its precious cargo would need to be pulled along. Archaeologists found the skeletons of about 12 horses nearby.

◁ *Some of the detailed carving on the Oseberg cart.*

Beautiful beds

Ordinary Vikings slept on benches or on the floor, so the beds found at Oseberg were further evidence that a rich woman was buried there. One of the five beds was in the front part of the ship, outside the burial chamber. Like the ship and cart, it was decorated with animal carvings. The other beds were inside. Two contained the skeletons and had tapestries made of silks and wools hung around them – more goods that ordinary Vikings could not have afforded to buy.

▽ *The tapestries from the Oseberg beds were damaged, but it is still possible to pick out the design of a cart being pulled along.*

Women and wealth

The Oseberg burial makes clear that Viking women were able to enjoy wealth and status. Even ordinary women whose husbands had gone 'a-viking' were allowed to run their farms. Women could also own land, and inherit it, too, but rarely did so if they had brothers or sons. They even had the right to divorce their husbands and to take half the goods that they had jointly owned.

Silent slaves

Documents such as law codes and travellers' accounts show historians that large numbers of slaves worked in Scandinavia during the Viking Age. However, archaeologists have found few objects that tell them about slaves' lives. It is not possible to tell which graves are those of slaves, while slaves buried with their owners often had no grave goods to accompany them on their journey. The Oseberg slave woman – if she was a slave – is certainly not able to speak clearly to us through the objects in her grave.

How society was governed

In the Viking homelands, society was governed by local **assemblies** called *Things*. They discussed important political matters, made laws and decided punishments for law-breaking. Every Viking freeman was allowed to attend and speak at these gatherings, which usually took place once a year.

As they settled in new places around the world, the Vikings often set up *Things* there, too. In fact, these assemblies remained important for longer in some settlements than in Scandinavia, where kings gradually took away much of their power.

Discovering Thingvellir

Thingvellir is a natural site in south-west Iceland. It was created thousands of years ago when hot, molten lava poured out of the Earth, then hardened to form spectacular rock shapes. The name Thingvellir means '**parliament** plains', and it was here that Viking Icelanders held the *Althing*, their national assembly. It took place for two weeks every June or July between 930 and 1271.

The freemen who took part in this national parliament, which was the first in Europe, came from thirteen district *Things*. They included the chieftain of each district, who was supposed to speak up for the rights and interests of his own people. Most chieftains could ride to Thingvellir on horseback in a day, but a few from eastern Iceland had to trek for seventeen days across difficult country.

WHO WAS Ari Thorgilsson?

Ari Thorgilsson, also known as Ari the Learned, was an Icelandic historian who lived from 1067 to 1148. His most famous work is 'The Book of Icelanders', which he wrote in about 1130. It tells the story of the Vikings in Iceland and provides important information about events that took place at Thingvellir. However, like other written works from the period, Ari's book is not completely reliable. Ari himself said that he based its contents on old stories told to him by his foster father, his uncle and a friend.

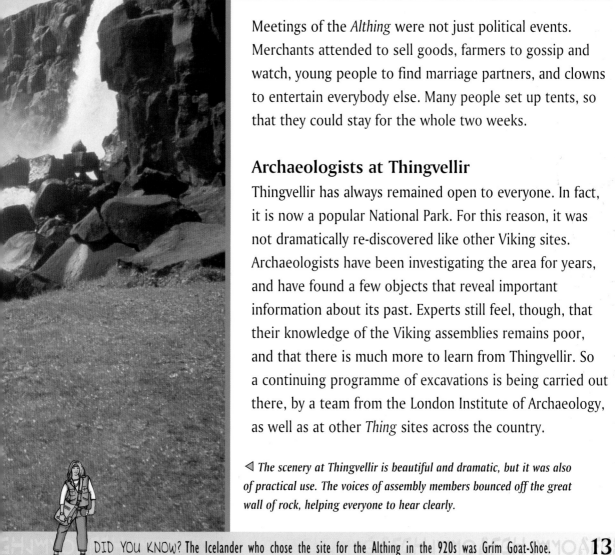

Meetings of the *Althing* were not just political events. Merchants attended to sell goods, farmers to gossip and watch, young people to find marriage partners, and clowns to entertain everybody else. Many people set up tents, so that they could stay for the whole two weeks.

Archaeologists at Thingvellir

Thingvellir has always remained open to everyone. In fact, it is now a popular National Park. For this reason, it was not dramatically re-discovered like other Viking sites. Archaeologists have been investigating the area for years, and have found a few objects that reveal important information about its past. Experts still feel, though, that their knowledge of the Viking assemblies remains poor, and that there is much more to learn from Thingvellir. So a continuing programme of excavations is being carried out there, by a team from the London Institute of Archaeology, as well as at other *Thing* sites across the country.

◁ *The scenery at Thingvellir is beautiful and dramatic, but it was also of practical use. The voices of assembly members bounced off the great wall of rock, helping everyone to hear clearly.*

Law, crime and punishment

Excavations at the Thingvellir site, together with research in books and documents, have already revealed important facts about how the Vikings governed themselves. In particular, they have shown how chieftains and ordinary freemen at the *Althing* and other assemblies made laws, punished crimes and reached major decisions.

The Law-Speaker and the Law Rock

A small group of people at the *Althing* was responsible for making Iceland's laws. It contained the 13 chieftains and 26 legal experts, two to advise each of the local leaders. The group was led by an official known as the Law-Speaker, who was elected every three years. It was his job to memorize all national laws, and to recite them aloud whenever the parliament met. To carry out this demanding task, the Law-Speaker stood in a special place at Thingvellir – on top of a huge piece of solidified lava known as the Law Rock.

Crimes and courts

In Viking society, there were frequent disputes between rival chieftains or other leaders. Often this led to violence, even murder. Men who had committed such crimes were usually judged by members of a *Thing*, and could be sent away from their homeland for ever as a punishment. As judgements, like laws, were rarely written down, legal experts tried to memorize them exactly.

Iceland also had five courts to consider serious crimes. Four had juries to decide whether a person was innocent or guilty. Judges in a special, fifth court ruled on very difficult cases. These often involved age-old, bitter clashes between the mightiest Viking chieftains and their families. Many of the **sagas** describe such complex legal battles.

Religion

Members of *Things* did
not concern themselves
only with crime. The most famous
decision made at the *Althing*, for
example, was about religion. By the 10th
century, some Icelanders had become
Christians, but others still worshipped
pagan gods. In 1000, the *Althing*
debated the subject and the Law-
Speaker announced the decision that
everyone should adopt Christianity.

EYEWITNESS

' "It seems to me good sense," he said,
"that ... we all have one law and custom; ...
if we divide the law, we will divide the
peace." Then Thorgeir [the Law-Speaker]
declared the law, that all ... people in the
land should become Christian...'

(From 'The Book of the Icelanders' by Ari Thorgilsson)

Bishops and crosiers

Gradually, Christianity replaced
paganism in all the Scandinavian
countries. As more people became
Christians, churches were built
and **bishops** were appointed. The
first bishop in Iceland was Isleif
Gissurarson, who was appointed in
1056. Then as now, bishops carried
long sticks, called **crosiers**, with a
cross or hook at the top. The
crosier shown on the left was
found at Birka, in Sweden.

Assemblies around the world

There were *Things* all over the Viking world and
modern place-names often provide a clue to
where they were. For example, Tingwall in the
Orkney Islands and Tynwald on the Isle of Man
(right) were both once sites of these
vigorous Viking assemblies.

The daily life of most Vikings involved a great deal of hard work. Men farmed their land and hunted to provide food for their families. Women looked after their children and houses, and cooked meals using the food that the men brought home.

Most ordinary Viking men were farmers. They kept cows, sheep, pigs, goats and chickens, and grew cereal crops, such as rye and barley, as well as many vegetables. A farmer's day began at daybreak and lasted until darkness fell again. Men went hunting and fishing, too, both to find extra food and for sport.

Viking women were based at home. Houses were rectangular and usually made of wood. Around the walls of the main room there were benches to sit or sleep on, and in the centre was a **hearth** (open fireplace) used for cooking and heating. Some houses had a separate area in which cows were kept, and it was the woman's job to milk them. Women also cared for the sick, using herbs and magic charms.

△ *Archaeologists discovered these Viking farm implements in Norway (from top to bottom): a scythe for cutting grass, a leaf-knife for cutting leaves for cows to eat, a sickle for harvesting cereals and a blade from a plough.*

Discovering Brattahlid

When the Vikings settled overseas, they often built farms there, too. In the late 10th century, Vikings led by Erik the Red arrived in Greenland from Iceland. They made their homes in two main places: the Eastern Settlement, where Erik built a farm called Brattahlid, and the Western Settlement, about 650 kilometres (404 miles) further north.

▷ *At Brattahlid, in Greenland, the Vikings built their settlement close to the coast where they arrived. The icebergs in the background are evidence of the cold climate.*

As the years passed, more and more Vikings came to this new colony, until there were many hundreds of farms. The farm buildings were not usually made from wood, as in Scandinavia, because Greenland has few trees. Instead, people generally built their homes from stones and **turf**. Experts believe that Viking settlement in Greenland came to an end during the 14th century.

Excavations at Brattahlid and other Greenland sites have helped **archaeologists** to learn much more about daily life in Viking times. The first excavations at Brattahlid were carried out by archaeologists from the National Museum of Denmark in 1932. They investigated a cluster of **ruins** that they believed might have been Erik the Red's own farm. In 1961, Danish archaeologists began further major work near this original site, after builders accidentally unearthed a Viking cemetery.

WHO WAS Erik the Red?

Erik the Red was a 10th-century Norwegian with a fiery temper. He had to leave his own country after a Thing found him guilty of murder. Next he settled in Iceland, where he married and began to build up a farm. But after more murders, he was sent away from that country, too. So, he left to found the Greenland colony. Erik is also famous as the father of Leif Eriksson, the Viking who in about 1000 founded a colony in North America.

Food and farming

A central hall

The cluster of buildings at Brattahlid that were excavated in 1932 had a rectangular, stone and turf hall at their heart. The walls of the hall were thick, to protect the people inside from Greenland's icy weather. Under the floor, there was a man-made channel through which water flowed into the house and at the centre there was a large hearth for cooking. Experts think that people in Brattahlid gathered in the hall to eat their evening meal.

Two meals a day

Vikings usually ate two meals a day: bread and porridge in the morning, and a heavy, meat-based dinner in the evening with large amounts of beer. In Scandinavia, the meat came from farm animals, such as cows, and wild animals, such as reindeer. The many animal bones that were discovered in Greenland showed archaeologists that Vikings there adapted to local conditions by also hunting and eating seals and caribou, a type of large deer.

Fantasy or Fact?

Experts are certain that Erik the Red lived at Brattahlid, but archaeology has shown that the hall and other ruins excavated in 1932 could not have belonged to him because they date from the 13th and 14th centuries. Older remains underneath the hall may have been his farm, but digs at the Viking cemetery in the 1960s and 1970s led to the discovery of another group of buildings that may have been his original home.

Relaxation

Having gathered in the Brattahlid hall for their evening meal, people would have listened to music, poems and stories from the **sagas**. They would also have enjoyed board games, including a Viking favourite called *hnefatafl*. It probably involved two players fighting 'wars' on a board. This is a playing piece from a *hnefatafl* game set.

Farm buildings

In Scandinavia, Viking farmers shared their homes with animals. This was true in Brattahlid, too. At one end of the hall there was a byre – a shelter for cows. Rooms for storing crops were also attached to the building, and there were four barns and two more byres near by. Byres contain partitions that keep the cows apart. In Brattahlid, these were made of stone or whale shoulder bones, as wood was scarce in Greenland.

△ *Sometimes archaeologists produce reconstructions to show how people lived in the past. Here, the knowledge archaeologists have gained from Viking remains and **artefacts** has been used to re-create a life-size model of a loom. The circular loom weights can be clearly seen at the bottom of the threads.*

Cloth and clothes

In one Brattahlid barn, archaeologists found a small, broken circular object with a hole in the middle. This was a stone **loom** weight. Viking weavers hung weights of this kind on the end of the vertical threads in the cloth they were making. In this way, they stopped the material becoming loose. Every Viking home contained a loom on which the women made fabric to turn into clothes.

People's clothes depended on how important they were. Most males wore shirts, short tunics and **breeches**, but the clothes of rich men were well-made from linen and fine wool, while poor men wore roughly woven, ill-fitting garments of coarse woollen cloth. Females usually wore full-length, long-sleeved tunics with long pinafores over the top, but the clothing of rich women was of better quality. Clothing was fastened with dress pins or brooches, made of bone, silver or bronze, depending on what could be afforded.

DID YOU KNOW? 'Brattahlid' means 'steep slope'.

TRADE AND TOWNS

Most Vikings were farmers, but many were traders who earned money by buying and selling. When not travelling abroad, these men usually spent their time in towns. There they met other merchants and bought trade goods from local craftspeople.

The Vikings were able to establish trading networks because they were expert sailors and built sturdy ships. These vessels allowed them to carry cargoes across the seas and along great European rivers, such as the Dneiper and Volga. They also succeeded because their homelands produced many desirable goods to sell, including furs, hunting falcons, **amber**, walrus **ivory** and iron. The Vikings traded in people, too, supplying slaves to eastern lands.

Viking traders bought as well as sold. Among the many goods they imported from Western Europe, Russia, the Middle East and Asia were silver, spices, wine and silks.

△ These coins from the Middle East and the Byzantine Empire were found in Viking burial sites in Sweden. They showed archaeologists that Viking traders had travelled far from Scandinavia.

Discovering Birka

The Swedes were perhaps the greatest Viking traders. From their homelands, they sailed east to Russia, the Arab World and the Byzantine Empire, in the area of modern Turkey. They established trading links with these regions, and with places even further afield, such as China.

WHO WAS Hjalmar Stolpe?

Hjalmar Stolpe trained not as an archaeologist, but as an entomologist (insect expert). When he went to Birka in 1871, his aim was to find prehistoric flies trapped in pieces of amber, but he soon realized that the town was a major Viking site. As well as excavating graves, Stolpe examined part of the 'Black Earth' area. Unlike many archaeologists of the time, who were little more than treasure-hunters, he worked as scientifically as he could.

△ *The remains of food, buildings and more have darkened the soil in the part of Birka where most people lived. Therefore it is called the 'Black Earth' area.*

As business increased, special trading towns grew up back in Sweden. One was Birka, which was founded in about 800 on an island called Björkö, at the edge of the Baltic Sea. Birka was home to foreign merchants and to native Swedes, both traders and craftspeople. Experts believe that no more than about 900 people ever lived there, but it would have been a busy, noisy place, full of men and women from many lands.

The importance of Birka was discovered thanks in particular to the work of one determined Swedish **archaeologist**, Hjalmar Stolpe. Starting in 1871, he **excavated** more than 1100 graves outside the town's walls and found many precious **grave goods**, including silver from the Middle East and silks from the Byzantine Empire.

There have been several more major digs at Birka since Stolpe's time. For long periods from the late 1960s to the mid-1990s, archaeological teams, led by Dr Björn Ambrosiani of Sweden's Museum of National Antiquities, have explored the 'Black Earth' area of Birka where most people lived.

Town life

The 1990s' digs in Birka's Black Earth area provided much information about day-to-day life in this important Swedish trading town. They also enabled experts to take a close-up look at workshops where men did metal-working, a craft at which Vikings excelled.

Homes by the harbour

Some of Sweden's trading centres grew up naturally, but Birka was a planned settlement, with houses and workshops enclosed inside a defensive wall and protected by a fort. The streets linking the Birka houses were very narrow, and many led down to small **jetties** that extended out into the harbour. When trading ships arrived, they moored next to the jetties, so that people could walk out to unload or examine goods.

Archaeology Challenge

Both during and since Viking times, the sea level around Birka has risen and fallen quite dramatically. This fact often makes it hard for archaeologists to work out exactly where to dig. In the late 1960s, Dr Björn Ambrosiani was trying to find the Viking town harbour. He knew that, in the 9th century, the sea had covered more of the island where Birka stands than it does now. So, instead of digging around the modern shoreline, he dug inland. He found a jetty on the first day that he started looking!

▽ *At this reconstructed Viking village, the houses have wattle-and-daub walls and turf roofs.*

Viking houses

*At Birka and in other parts of Scandinavia, house frameworks were made of sturdy wooden posts. The posts were joined together with either woven twigs, called wattle, or planks. If wattle was used, it was coated with daub, a sticky mixture of clay, dung and water, which dried to make it waterproof. This type of construction is known as wattle-and-daub. Roofs were made of wood, thatch or **turf**.*

Craft workshops

Many of Sweden's trading towns and other centres contained craft workshops. Some produced jewellery and other goods for merchants to sell abroad, but many craft items from Birka were probably given to local farmers in exchange for food, as little could be produced in the town itself.

The 1990s' excavations revealed much more about the town's workshops, where a wide variety of metal objects were made. Workshop rooms were small, with wattle-and-daub walls and **hearths** around the sides. It was important to keep the hearth fires burning, as they were used for melting metal. Experts think that screens were probably placed in front of them to stop draughts.

From clay to bronze

Viking metalworkers made tools and weapons from iron, and jewellery from gold, silver and bronze. Objects, such as this bronze brooch, were made by first creating clay moulds (below). While the clay was soft, an object that already had the required shape was pressed on to it, to transfer the pattern. After the moulds had dried hard, hot bronze was poured inside. The bronze then cooled and hardened, so that by the time the mould was opened, it had taken on the pattern in the clay.

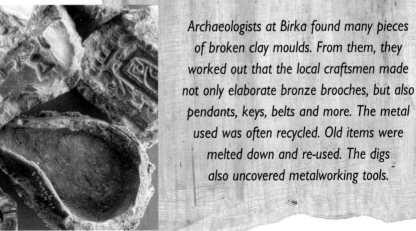

Archaeologists at Birka found many pieces of broken clay moulds. From them, they worked out that the local craftsmen made not only elaborate bronze brooches, but also pendants, keys, belts and more. The metal used was often recycled. Old items were melted down and re-used. The digs also uncovered metalworking tools.

VIKINGS AT WAR

Vikings were expert and eager warriors. Rival chieftains and their followers fought each other, at home and abroad. Hit-and-run **raiders** attacked coastal **monasteries** and villages across northwestern Europe. And mighty armies, seeking conquest as well as treasure, waged long and brutal wars against foreign enemies.

△ *In 878 the Anglo-Saxons pushed the Vikings out of Wessex and part of Mercia. The areas north and east of the red line were controlled by the Vikings and became known as the Danelaw.*

When Vikings arrived in Greenland they faced no opposition, as no one else lived there. However, when they decided to settle in England, the Vikings first had to conquer its **Anglo-Saxon** inhabitants. Viking **campaigns** against the English began in earnest in 866, when a powerful group of fighting men, who became known as the Great Army, arrived from Denmark. By 874 the Vikings controlled all of England except for the kingdom of Wessex. In 878 the people of Wessex, led by King Alfred the Great, defeated the Vikings at the Battle of Edington, forcing them to return to northern and eastern England. These Viking-ruled territories became known as the Danelaw.

Discovering Repton

In summer, the Great Army moved around England from battle to battle. Then, as the weather became cold and unsuitable for fighting, they built camps for the winter. In 1974, **archaeologists** discovered by chance the remains of a Viking winter camp at Repton in Derbyshire.

Repton was also the site of an Anglo-Saxon church and monastery, where monks once lived. It was this site that archaeologists Birthe and Martin Biddle were **excavating** when they discovered the remains of an earth bank with a ditch alongside. The bank and ditch swept in a semi-circle down to the River Trent, which joined the two ends of the curve to create a D shape. The archaeologists knew that the Danes built **enclosures** in this shape for protection.

△ Remains of a bank and ditch at Repton were evidence that Vikings had set up camp there.

Excavations at Repton continued until 1988 and confirmed that the Great Army had almost certainly spent the winter of 873 to 874 there. They also showed that the **pagan** Viking soldiers had seized the church from its Christian inhabitants and built the defensive earth bank around it.

WHO WAS Rollo?

Like England, France was the target of campaigns by Viking armies. The most famous of these armies was led by a Norwegian known as Rollo. In 911 the ruler of France, Charles the Simple, tried to persuade Rollo to stop his attacks by giving him land in the north of the country. Rollo took the land – but carried on fighting. Many Vikings settled on Rollo's land and adopted the French language and way of life. They became known as Normans and their land as Normandy. These were the Normans who invaded and conquered England in 1066.

DID YOU KNOW? A school and playing fields now stand on the site of the Repton winter camp.

Warriors and weapons

Hundreds of skeletons were found at the Repton site. The most revealing belonged to a warrior who had died in battle. However, it was hard to discover who many of the others were or what had killed them.

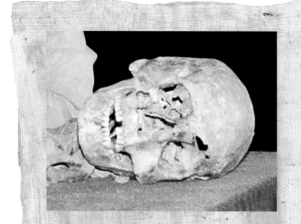

Death of a fighting man

Viking graves were scattered around the church at Repton, including one belonging to a man aged about 40. Examination of his bones showed that a savage blow to the hip had caused his death.

There were many items in the grave with the skeleton. A silver pendant shaped like a hammer was hanging around the neck of the skull. The hammer was the symbol of Thor, the Viking god of thunder, who was believed to fight giants and demons. Weapons in the grave, including a sword, scabbard (sword-holder) and a selection of knives, made it clear the man was a warrior.

Weapons and armour

Every non-slave Viking had the right to own weapons, but the quality and type of the weapon depended on a man's status. Professional soldiers and rich men always had at least one long, sometimes decorated, sword with a double cutting edge of sharp steel. They also carried knives, which could kill an enemy close at hand, and spears, which could be thrust into an enemy from a distance. Some also had simple, metal-bladed battleaxes, but these were more often the weapons of ordinary working men who did not fight often.

Armour

In battle, many high-ranking men wore padded jackets under tunics made of chain mail (linked metal rings). They also had large, round, wooden shields and pointed iron helmets with protective metal bands covering the nose and cheeks. The front of this helmet, found in a boat grave in Sweden, is protected by chain mail. Ordinary fighting men had helmets and shields but little else.

Mass burial mystery

In 1986, archaeologists excavated the site of a former Anglo-Saxon chapel just outside Repton's D-shaped bank. There they found a mass grave, with the remains of 249 people that the Vikings had buried inside it. One man had been buried on his own in the middle, suggesting that he was a chieftain, but unfortunately his skeleton had already been removed.

Coins discovered in the grave suggest that it was dug when the Great Army was in Repton, but the bones showed that the men had not died in battle. About one-fifth of the skeletons belonged to women, perhaps Anglo-Saxon wives of Viking men, and they had not died in fighting either. Experts' best guess is that disease swept through the camp and surrounding areas in the winter of 873 to 874, killing many of the people. But the identity of the missing chieftain remains a mystery.

Fantasy or Fact?

The warrior's grave by the church in Repton contained a small bag with a bird bone and a boar tusk inside. These animal remains may have had some practical use, but experts believe that they were probably charms designed to keep away evil.

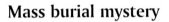

SHIPS AND SEAFARING

Without their superb ships, the Vikings could not have made the impact on the world that they did, either as warriors or as traders. The Vikings showed that they valued their sea-going craft by burying important people in ships, for example at Oseberg, and by sometimes arranging stones on graves in boat shapes. They also carved pictures of ships, for example at Gotland.

△ These stones marking graves in Lindholm Høje, Denmark, are arranged in boat shapes.

Archaeologists began to discover the remains of Viking ships in the 19th century. In 1880, a ship 23 metres (75 feet) long was unearthed from a burial mound in Gokstad, Norway. It had been built in about 850, possibly as a royal barge, and then become the grave of a king. The craft was built from oak planks and had holes in the sides to hold 16 pairs of oars. Its sail was made of red and white fabric strips that could be hung downwards or interwoven to make a check pattern.

Three smaller boats were also found in the burial mound, telling archaeologists more about everyday Viking ships, such as fishing boats. More information was revealed by the Oseberg burial in 1904. However, it was many years later before experts had the chance to examine a far greater variety of Viking vessels at a single site, Roskilde **Fjord** in Denmark.

△ This ship was discovered in a burial mound in Gokstad, Norway.

Discovering Roskilde

In the 11th century, Denmark and Norway were at war. To keep the Norwegians out of Roskilde, then Denmark's capital, the Danes blocked the fjord that led up to it by deliberately sinking five ships. The fjord area where the ships went down was called Skuldelev.

About 900 years later, in 1956, divers found a strangely shaped piece of oak in Skuldelev's shallow waters. It proved to be the mast of a Viking ship and led Danish archaeologist and ship expert Dr Ole Crumlin-Pedersen to begin underwater excavations.

The archaeological team eventually found all five of the ships that had been sunk, and lifted them slowly and gently from the seabed. After so many years in water, the craft were damaged and had soft, soggy timbers. Even so, it was clear that this was a major find. The experts had discovered two types of warship, a ferry and two merchant ships for carrying cargo. They were able to rebuild four of the craft, but one warship was too damaged to reconstruct.

Archaeology Challenge

Working underwater poses special problems. When engineers have to work in water to build a bridge, they construct **enclosures** called cofferdams on the sea- or riverbed. Then they pump all the water out so that they can work inside without getting too wet. Archaeologists at Roskilde used exactly the same technique to help them find and recover the Viking ships.

△ *The cofferdam around the excavation site at Roskilde was built in 1962, six years after the first discovery there.*

Shipbuilding and navigation

Examination of the ships found at Roskilde and other sites helped archaeologists understand more about Viking vessels and how they were built. Other discoveries led them to think closely about how Vikings found their way across the oceans to distant lands.

Warships

One of the Roskilde warships was too light to be a true Viking **longship**, but the other, the vessel that could not be rebuilt, was of exactly the type that struck fear into people's hearts as they saw it approach. In its original state, this ship measured 30 metres (100 feet) from prow (front) to stern (back). It was powered by the wind in its single sail and by 36 oarsmen, 18 on each side. They would have hung their colourful shields over the side as they rowed.

Merchant ships

The two merchant ships found at Roskilde were wider and shorter than the warships. One was a **knorr**, designed to carry heavy cargoes across open oceans. The other (right) was of a lighter type, for use in shallow coastal waters and rivers.

Shipbuilding – special features of Viking ships

All Viking ships were clinker-built, that is, made of slightly overlapping wooden planks. Rivets (metal pins) held the planks together. Commonly used woods were oak and pine. The **hulls** of the ships were not very deep and this made it possible for Viking warriors to sail up to a beach, rather than anchoring out to sea like other vessels. This tactic terrified people under attack on land, who did not realize how close the longships could get until it was too late.

Another important feature of Viking ships was the giant rudders attached under the water at the back. By turning a handle attached to these blades, warriors could steer the ships accurately.

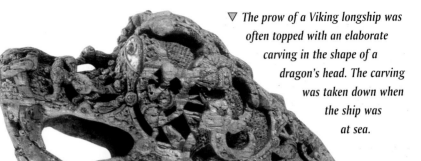

▽ *The prow of a Viking longship was often topped with an elaborate carving in the shape of a dragon's head. The carving was taken down when the ship was at sea.*

◁ *In 1984, the Saga Siglar, a replica of one of the Roskilde ships, sailed around the world. On the voyage, the sailors tested the 'Sun compass'.*

Navigation skills

Viking sailors learned how to use the positions of the Sun and stars and the direction of the wind to judge where they were and where they were going. They were also skilled at estimating how far and how fast they had travelled. Some people have suggested that the Vikings also had simple tools for **navigation**. In Greenland during the 1940s, an archaeologist found half of what had been a circular wooden object. It had a hole in the middle and notches around the edge. When Danish sailor Captain C.V. Sølver saw it, he suggested it was a form of compass that used the angle of the Sun's rays to show a ship's direction. Trials of this 'Sun compass' showed that it worked, but many experts believe that the Vikings never used it.

Vikings around the world

The Vikings travelled far and wide. There is clear archaeological evidence that they reached Russia in the east, but experts were unsure about tales in the **sagas** that the Vikings also reached North America in the west. Different sagas tell different stories about the Vikings in North America, but experts have tried to work out from them what really happened. They think that the first Viking to see the coast of North America was Bjarni Herjolfsson, who ended up there by mistake while trying to reach Greenland. Later, Leif Eriksson set out to find the land Bjarni had sailed past. He did so in about 1000, and called the region 'Vinland' ('Wineland') – perhaps because he saw grapes there. Some experts think they were probably a type of berry.

▷ *The houses at L'Anse-aux-Meadows were made from driftwood covered with turf.*

Fantasy or Fact?

In 1965 Yale, one of the best universities in the USA, published a map. It was said to show Vinland and to date from the mid-15th century. As it was thought to be based on a Viking map, it seemed to prove that the Vikings had been to North America. Many Viking Age experts were impressed by this document. However, scientific tests in the 1970s showed that it was a forgery. The ink used to draw its shaky outlines was first made in the 20th century.

Leif Eriksson and his companions built **turf** shelters in Vinland, but stayed only for the winter. A few years later, an Icelander called Thorfinn Karlsefni tried to create a permanent farming settlement there. However, bad relations with Native Americans, and the difficulty of obtaining supplies from their homelands, led the Vikings to leave after about three years.

Discovering L'Anse-aux-Meadows

The sagas did not say where in North America Eriksson had landed. The north-east coast seemed a likely place, but grapes had never grown in this cold region. Sadly, there seemed to be no Viking sites to help solve this puzzle. Then, in 1960, Norwegian explorer Helge Ingstad heard about possible Viking remains in L'Anse-aux-Meadows, Newfoundland, an island off the east coast of Canada. He and his wife, archaeologist Anne Stine Ingstad, set out to investigate.

Working from 1961 to 1968, the Ingstads found a cluster of eight turf and **driftwood** houses with the remains of **hearths** and benches inside, in the exact style of Viking homes. They also found Viking-style objects, including a bronze pin and a **spindle** part. Icelandic archaeologists working with the Ingstads **excavated** a **forge** on the site and found a **kiln**, rivets and other evidence of metalworking. The Ingstads were now convinced that they had found the only known Viking site in North America, and in the 1970s a Swedish team of archaeologists confirmed their view. However, whether this cold, grape-free area is the Vinland of the sagas may remain unclear forever.

Archaeology Challenge

Living things, like plants and animals, absorb from the air a **radioactive** type of the chemical carbon, called Carbon-14. When they die, this carbon decays at a rate that experts know and can measure. As a result, the age of bone, wood, or anything else that once formed part of a living thing, can be found by analysing how much Carbon-14 it contains. Experts used this technique, called radiocarbon dating, to work out the age of the L'Anse-aux-Meadows site. They found that it dated from Viking times.

DID YOU KNOW? L'Anse-aux-Meadows comes from the site's original French name, meaning 'Jellyfish Creek'. **33**

ART, LEARNING AND RELIGION

The Vikings were practical people, who liked to sail, farm and trade. They also had cultural and spiritual interests, creating beautiful objects, writing powerful literature and practising their faith, whether **pagan** or Christian. Finds from many sites demonstrate these interests in art, learning and religion.

Discovering Gotland

Gotland is an island in the Baltic Sea, off the coast of Sweden. In Viking times, as now, its rich land was covered in farms. In addition, as it can be reached easily from other Baltic islands, the Scandinavian mainland, Poland and Russia, Gotland was a centre of trade.

Evidence of the island's trading links comes from the many coins and other treasures found there. In 1999, for example, two **hoards** were discovered in a single field. They contained 70 kilograms of silver items, including jewellery and Arab coins.

Gotland is important to **archaeologists** for another reason, too. Its people had a thriving cultural life that, although clearly Viking, was unlike anything else in Scandinavia.

Fantasy or Fact?

*Archaeologists and others have found hundreds of treasure hoards on Gotland, but they are not sure why. Some think that the islanders were pirates who stole these precious goods from ships. Others believe that the islanders were frightened of pirates, so hid valuable belongings under the ground. A third theory is that the islanders buried their possessions for religious reasons. They may have been saving them for the afterlife or **sacrificing** them to the gods.*

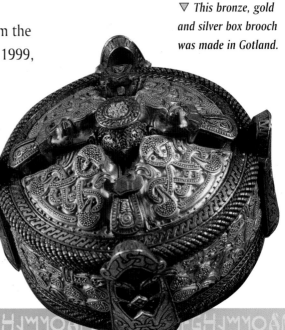

▽ *This bronze, gold and silver box brooch was made in Gotland.*

▷ These iron-working and carpentry tools were found in a bog at Mästermyr on Gotland.

In addition, they produced huge numbers of goods. There are more pre-Viking and Viking objects on Gotland, an island of 3000 square kilometres, than there are in Sweden itself, which is about 150 times as large.

Marvellous metalwork

Gotland's metalwork has attracted special interest. Even practical items, such as metal fittings on horse harnesses, were decorated with intertwined animals and birds. The island's jewellery was more striking still. The unique, circular box brooches, for example, were covered in beautiful filigree – strands of gold or other metal twisted into intricate shapes.

The swirling animals on Gotland metalwork were copied on the wooden prow of the Oseberg ship, but in a different style. Later, the Oseberg animals were copied, again in a slightly different way. This process continued throughout the Viking Age, so by looking at the precise style of a piece of metalwork or other art, experts can tell when it was produced.

Picture stones

Despite the beauty of its metalwork, Gotland is famous above all for something else unique – its picture stones. Experts have found about 370 of these carved blocks from the Viking Age and earlier. They were designed as memorials, and are covered in pictures of people, ships and scenes from **myths**.

▷ The Gotland picture stones are a wonderful source of information about Viking times.

DID YOU KNOW? Fish-shaped pendants were another item of Viking jewellery made only in Gotland. **35**

Gods and goddesses

The Vikings' pagan religion included many gods and goddesses, but it is hard to work out exactly what people believed or how they worshipped. For help, experts turn to sources such as the Gotland picture stones and writings called Eddas.

There are two Eddas, both compiled in Iceland during the 13th century. The *Poetic Edda* contains 39 poems from many periods and several countries. Ten are about the gods of Viking

religion. The *Prose Edda* was put together by Snorri Sturluson. It was designed to help young writers compose new poetry and understand the references to gods and goddesses in existing poetry. As it contains retellings of all the Viking myths, it is very useful to people who want to understand Viking religion.

Picture stories

The Gotland picture stones were carved from the 5th century AD until the end of the Viking Age. It is possible to follow the development of Scandinavian religion through their pictures. The pre-Viking stones often feature a wheel (above). Some experts believe this represents the Sun – evidence that the islanders long ago worshipped this star. The later stones, carved by Vikings, show many of their pagan gods, including the mighty trio of Odin, Thor and Freyr. Also portrayed is Valhalla, the great hall thought to be the resting place of Viking warriors who died in battle. The last stones come from the time when Christianity was replacing paganism. Many of them are marked with a cross.

▽ *This scene from a picture stone tells a story from the* Prose Edda *about a blacksmith. The hammers and tongs that he used for his work can be seen near the top right of the image.*

The Final Day

Viking mythology did not promise a happy end for the gods. It foretold that they would all die on the Final Day, called Ragnarök, and that the whole world would be destroyed by fire.

Fantasy or Fact?

Little is known about the places where the Vikings worshipped their gods. However, an 11th-century German Christian, called Adam of Bremen, did write a description of a temple that he saw in Uppsala, Sweden. According to him, there were statues of Odin, Thor and Freyr inside the temple, and both animals and men were sacrificed to them. As a Christian, Adam would probably have been eager to criticize pagan rituals. But modern experts think that sacrifice really did form a part of Viking religious practice.

The Viking gods

The stories of the Viking gods originally came from Germany and other parts of central Europe. There were many versions, but the most powerful and widely worshipped gods appear in them all.

The Viking gods were said to live in a place called Asgard. Odin was the chief among them and was a sinister character who did powerful magic. He also helped warriors and welcomed them to Valhalla, his home, after death. Odin rode an eight-legged horse, Sleipnir.

The figure on the left is of Thor, another powerful god. He was thought to be more sympathetic to ordinary people. He carried a hammer to defend Asgard and ruled over the sky, often causing storms.

Freyr and his sister Freyia were **fertility** gods. They were responsible for ensuring that people had many children and that the land produced plentiful crops. Some farmers even called their fields after Freyr, in the hope that this would ensure a good harvest.

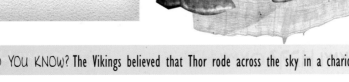

The arrival of Christianity

The pagan beliefs of the Vikings remained strong throughout the 9th century. But, gradually, contact with countries outside their Scandinavian homelands, and the arrival of **missionaries** in Scandinavia, led to the spread of a very different faith – Christianity. The first major missionary to the Vikings was Ansgar, a monk from Germany. He travelled to Denmark and Sweden in the mid-9th century, and founded churches in places such as Birka. However, people did not immediately **convert** to Christianity in large numbers.

More than 100 years later, in about 960, King Harald Bluetooth introduced the new religion in Denmark. Then, in the early 11th century, King Olaf Haraldsson forced Norway to accept it. By that time, Norwegian missionaries had already taken Christianity to Iceland, where the *Althing* adopted it in 1000. Leif Eriksson carried the faith to Greenland a short while later. In Sweden, pagan resistance was strong, and so Christianity did not become widespread there until the late 11th century.

EYEWITNESS

'King Olaf laid such stress on all men in his kingdom being Christians that he offered them the choice: be killed, leave the country or take baptism.'

(An account from a saga explaining how Olaf Haraldsson persuaded Norwegian pagans to convert to Christianity)

▷ *These are the ruins of Gardar Cathedral in Greenland. When still standing, it was more than 30 metres (98 feet) long. Gardar was one of the earliest major Christian sites in the Viking world.*

Discovering Jelling

Jelling was once the home of the kings of Denmark, and is a key site in the story of Christianity's arrival in that country. Archaeologists revealed this story by **excavating** two burial mounds, as well as a church and two **rune** stones that stand between them. The tale concerns the Danish king Gorm, who in the 930s refused to accept Christianity, his wife Thyri and his son Harald Bluetooth.

▽ *Rune stones are stones with Viking letters (runes) on them. The rune stones at Jelling stand just outside the church.*

It was widely believed that the North Mound at Jelling contained the body of Queen Thyri. When excavations began there in 1820, experts hoped to confirm this. However, although the mound contained a 10th-century burial chamber, there were no human remains. There were just animal bones and **grave goods**. Excavations of the South Mound, Gorm's supposed burial place, in the 1860s and 1940s, were even less helpful – they found nothing at all.

Archaeologists' luck began to improve in the mid-1960s, when Dr Knud Krogh from the National Museum of Denmark began to excavate the church. He showed that, over time, there had been three separate churches on the site, and he found a grave under the floor of the oldest. It dated from the mid-10th century, when Harald Bluetooth was on the throne, and contained the skeleton of a man, some jewellery and some golden threads.

Archaeologists now had the finds to help them tell the story, but they also had other important evidence. It came from the rune stones.

Runes and writing

Runes were the letters of the Viking alphabet, and Vikings used them to carve messages on stone, wood, bone and metal. Archaeologists use the runic writings to help them solve puzzles of the past, like the story of Jelling.

The Jelling story

From studying the rune stones, experts now believe that the pagan king Gorm was buried in the North Mound, but that his bones were removed by his son, Harald Bluetooth. As the larger rune stone states, the Danes converted to Christianity during Harald's reign and, as a Christian, Harald would have wanted to rebury his father in the church. This means that the bones found there are likely to be Gorm's.

Experts still do not know where Thyri is buried. As the smaller rune stone is a memorial to her, it seems likely that her grave was nearby, possibly in the South Mound.

The Jelling stones

The larger rune stone at Jelling has three sides, all of them carved with intertwining, Viking-style designs. One side also carries a picture of Jesus on the cross (above). The runic message is long, but its main words are: 'King Harald had this memorial made for Gorm his father and Thyri his mother. It was this Harald who ... made the Danes Christians.' The other rune stone is much smaller, and the writing on it declares: 'King Gorm made this memorial to his wife Thyri, Denmark's glory'.

The runic alphabet

Runes were used right across the Viking world, but are especially common in Sweden. By the Viking Age, there were two runic alphabets, with 16 symbols in each. The short-twig alphabet was the main form in Norway and Sweden, and the long-branch alphabet in Denmark, but sometimes the two were mixed. Both were used above all for memorials, as at Jelling, but there are also runic charms and graffiti. Runic writing began to die out after the arrival of Christianity from Western Europe, as this led to the gradual introduction of the **Roman alphabet**.

▷ *The Rök stone in Ostergötland, Sweden, has the longest known runic inscription.*

Skalds and sagas

When Vikings gathered to enjoy a meal, men called skalds often entertained them by reciting poems, for example about Viking history or in honour of a listening leader. Skalds usually memorized these works, but sometimes wrote them down in runes. After the Roman alphabet arrived, most skalds put their poems in books instead.

The **saga**-writers also wrote in the Roman alphabet, and used both information and quotations from skaldic writings.

Fantasy or Fact?

According to Viking mythology, the god Odin discovered runes. In fact, people began to use these symbols, which are all made up of straight lines, in pre-Viking times. Experts think the lack of curves was deliberate, as it makes runes easy to carve in wood, stone, or other hard material.

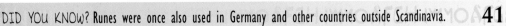

From the 19th century to the present, **archaeologists** have made major finds all over the Viking world. Their work has enabled historians to build up a more accurate picture of this world and its people than was possible before, when they could rely only on **sagas** and guesswork.

Over the past two centuries, **archaeology** has changed in many ways. In the early days, it was often a pastime for rich men, who wanted above all to find glittering treasures – fast. Gradually, it has become a serious field of study in which science plays an important part, and evidence is slowly and carefully gathered. Increasingly, too, archaeologists are as interested in the lives and possessions of ordinary workers as of kings, queens and **nobles**. These general changes in archaeology have had particular effects at Viking sites. At Birka, Hjalmar Stolpe pioneered the use of careful excavation. At L'Anse-aux-Meadows, the scientific technique of radiocarbon dating combined with excavation to prove that Vikings reached North America. And at places as different as Repton and Gotland, experts have tried to find out what everyday life was like for ordinary people. Today, excavations are continuing all over the Viking world.

Lake Tissø

At Lake Tissø in Denmark, archaeologists are digging up a huge manor house. Interest in the area began in 1977, when a beautiful gold necklace was unearthed there. A team from the Danish National Museum, led by Lars Jørgensen, finally started the first of many digs at the site in 1995. Over

△ *These finely made silver and bronze jewellery pieces are among the many treasures found at Tissø.*

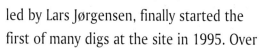

10,000 objects have been found, including exquisite items of jewellery. Their high quality suggests that the manor house was once used by kings, but probably only as a temporary residence for feasts and celebrations. The discovery of many miniature sculptures of the god Thor's hammer symbol indicates that the manor was also a centre for religious rituals.

The Fröjel Discovery Programme

Fröjel is a harbour in Gotland where excavations began in 1998. The archaeologists are trying to find out more about the layout of the harbour and neighbouring settlement, and about the area's trade links with other parts of the world. By excavating the local church and graveyards, they are also hoping to learn when and how Christianity was introduced in the area.

▽ *Visitors to Fröjel, Gotland, take part in the archaeological project to excavate graves.*

The excavations are part of the Fröjel Discovery Programme, which aims to involve ordinary people in archaeological projects. Some digs are opento the general public and to schoolchildren, and foreign students are encouraged to visit.

When the digs are over, the site will become a visitor centre, both to provide jobs and to let people enjoy the benefits of archaeologists' hard work for years to come.

Some of the dates in this timeline have a small letter 'c' in front of them. This stands for 'circa', a Latin word meaning 'about', and indicates that these dates are approximate.

793

In the first known Viking raid, Norwegians attack a monastery on Lindisfarne in north-east England.

9th century

An elaborate ship burial of two women takes place in Oseberg, Norway.

c 800

The Viking trading colony of Birka is founded on the Swedish island of Björkö.

829–831

Ansgar, a German monk, journeys to Denmark and to Birka in Sweden to try to convert people to Christianity.

850s

Ansgar makes further missionary visits to Scandinavia.

The Viking ship found at Gokstad by 19th-century archaeologists is built.

866

The Viking Great Army arrives in England from Denmark.

c 870–930

Vikings from Norway and elsewhere establish a settlement in Iceland.

c 873–874

The Danish Great Army camps at Repton in Derbyshire, England. Many soldiers and others die in an epidemic.

878

Alfred the Great defeats the Viking Great Army at the Battle of Edington. England is then divided between the western part, under Alfred's rule, and the northeastern part, controlled by the Vikings (the Danelaw).

911

Charles the Simple, king of France, grants Norwegian Vikings an area of northern France. It becomes known as Normandy.

930–1271

The *Althing* (national assembly) meets every summer in Thingvellir, Iceland.

c 958

Danish King Gorm is buried at Jelling.

958–987

King Harald Bluetooth, Gorm's son, rules Denmark and in about 960 begins to introduce Christianity there.

c 960 and c 980

Erik the Red is forced to leave first Norway and then Iceland as a punishment for murder.

c 985

Erik the Red settles in Greenland and establishes a Viking community there.

c 985–986

Bjarni Herjolfsson probably becomes the first Viking to see the coast of North America when blown off course on a voyage to Greenland.

1000

Leif Eriksson, son of Erik the Red, founds a short-lived Viking colony in North America and calls it Vinland.

Icelandic Vikings adopt Christianity.

c 1005

Icelandic Viking Thorfinn Karlsefni creates a more permanent settlement in North America after the departure of Leif Eriksson. But the hostility of the Native Americans and the difficulty of obtaining supplies from Iceland cause the settlers to leave after three years.

1014

Olaf Haraldsson becomes King of Norway and begins to convert the country to Christianity.

1066

The descendants of Norwegian Vikings who settled in Normandy, France, in 911 invade England. After defeating King Harold II, William the Conqueror, their leader, becomes England's ruler.

1067–1148

Life of Icelandic historian Ari the Learned.

11th century

Denmark and Norway become united Christian countries ruled by strong kings and the Viking Age ends there.

12th century

Sweden becomes the last Viking country to develop a stable, Christian monarchy and the whole Viking Age draws to a close.

13th century

Life of Icelandic historian and saga writer Snorri Sturluson.

The *Poetic Edda* and the *Prose Edda* are compiled in Iceland.

TIMELINE OF VIKING ARCHAEOLOGY

1820

Archaeologists excavate the North Mound in Jelling, Denmark, hoping to find the remains of Thyri, a 10th-century queen. They find only animal bones and grave goods.

1860s

Archaeologists at Jelling's South Mound look for the remains of King Gorm, Thyri's husband, but find nothing.

1871

Swedish archaeologist Hjalmar Stolpe begins excavations in the Viking trading colony of Birka, Sweden. He discovers 1100 graves and impressive grave goods from around the world.

1880

Archaeologists, led by Nicolay Nicolaysen, President of the Antiquarian Society in Oslo, Norway, excavate a burial mound in Gokstad. The Viking ships they uncover include one in which a king was buried.

1904

Gabriel Gustafsson, a Swedish professor and director of the University Museum in the Norwegian city of Oslo, leads the team that excavates the ship burial in Oseberg, Norway.

1932

Archaeologists from the National Museum of Denmark carry out the first excavations at Brattahlid, Greenland, where Norwegian Viking Erik the Red established a farming settlement during the 10th century.

1940s

Further excavations at Jelling's North Mound produce no significant finds.

1956

Divers discover the remains of a Viking sailing ship in Roskilde Fjord, Denmark. Danish archaeologist Dr Ole Crumlin-Pedersen begins excavations, finding five different Viking ships.

1961–68

Archaeologist Anne Stine Ingstad and explorer Helge Ingstad, her husband, excavate the remains of a Viking settlement in L'Anse-aux-Meadows, Newfoundland. They attempt to show that it is the site of Leif Eriksson's Vinland.

1965

Yale University in the USA publishes the 'Vinland Map', which is said to prove that the Vikings visited North America.

Mid-1960s

Dr Knud Krogh from the National Museum of Denmark leads new excavations at Jelling and discovers a grave under the church. The human bones it contained are probably those of King Gorm.

1960s–1970s

Dr Knud Krogh leads more excavations at Brattahlid in Greenland.

1960s–1990s

Dr Björn Ambrosiani from Sweden's Museum of National Antiquities leads excavations in the Viking trading colony of Birka.

1970s

A team of Swedish archaeologists continues work in L'Anse-aux-Meadows. They agree that it is a Viking settlement.

The 'Vinland Map' is shown to be a forgery.

1974–88

Archaeologists Birthe and Martin Biddle discover and excavate a Viking enclosure in Repton, England. It proves to be the site of a winter camp used by the Danish Great Army.

1977

A Viking necklace made of gold and weighing 1.8 kg (4 lb) is unearthed at Lake Tissø in Denmark.

1986

Archaeologists working at Repton discover a mass grave outside the Viking enclosure. The remains inside probably belong to people who died of disease rather than in battle.

1995

Lars Jørgensen, an archaeologist from the Danish National Museum, begins excavations on the site of a Viking manor house at Lake Tissø in Denmark (see also 1977 above). So far, about 10,000 Viking objects have been discovered there.

1998

Archaeologists begin to excavate the Viking harbour of Fröjel on the Swedish island of Gotland. In the 21st century, they are still working there as part of the Fröjel Discovery Programme.

1999

Two huge coin hoards from the Viking era are found on Gotland.

2002–2006

Experts from Iceland's Institute of Archaeology plan excavations at the *Althing* site of Thingvellir.

amber

A clear, orange-brown, hard substance that formed from liquid that oozed out of ancient trees. Amber pieces are often used to make jewellery.

Anglo-Saxon

(Of or relating to) the people who were the main inhabitants of England when the Vikings arrived. They were descendants of the Angles, Saxons and other tribes who had moved to England from Germany.

archaeologist

A person who studies the past by examining and scientifically analysing old objects and ruins.

artefacts

An object made by humans, especially an ancient object discovered by archaeologists.

assembly

A group of people formally gathered for a particular purpose, for example to discuss politics or make laws.

baptism

Ceremony where water is placed on a person's forehead, or they are immersed in water, as a sign that Jesus Christ has washed their sins away and they have become a Christian.

bishop

A senior Christian priest who governs one of the dioceses (districts) into which the Christian Church is divided.

breeches

Leg coverings that extend from the waist to the knee. Vikings often wound strips of cloth around the lower part of their legs, from knee to ankle, to keep them warm and dry.

campaign

A series of battles and other activities designed to achieve a long-term military aim, for example conquering a particular country.

cells

The tiny pieces of matter from which every part of the human body is made. DNA is contained in the central area of each cell called the nucleus.

convert

To change, or cause someone to change, religious beliefs.

crosier

A stick with a cross or hook at the top, similar to the sticks once carried by shepherds. Bishops carry crosiers as a sign of their duty to look after Christians as shepherds care for sheep.

driftwood

Pieces of wood washed up on the seashore or the edge of a lake.

enclosure

An area of land, water or both, surrounded by a ditch, wall or other barrier.

excavate

To dig up (a building or area of land) in order to look for ancient objects, ruins or other evidence of the past.

fertility

(Of people) the ability to have children; (of land) the ability to produce good crops.

fjord

A narrow area of water that extends inland from the coast and has high cliffs on either side.

forge

The workplace of a blacksmith. There metal is heated to make it soft, then beaten into new shapes, for example to make tools and weapons.

freemen

Men who belonged to the class of Vikings between royalty and nobility at the top and slaves at the bottom.

grave goods

Objects buried with a body in a grave. They are often precious items that the person owned when alive and wanted to keep with them after death.

hearth

A fireplace, especially one that is on the floor in the middle of a room.

hoard

A hidden stock (of treasure).

hull

The main body of a ship, part of which is above and part below water when the ship is sailing along.

ivory

The hard, cream-coloured material from which walrus and elephant tusks are made.

jetty (plural jetties)

A small pier that sticks out into the sea or other area of water.

kiln

A type of oven in which newly made pottery is dried and hardened.

knorr

A wide, deep type of Viking ship used for carrying cargo. Knorrs had both a sail and oars.

longship

A narrow, shallow type of Viking ship with a high, curved stem (front) and stern (back). Viking warriors went on raids in longships, which had both a sail and oars.

loom

A large, often upright frame on which strands of wool, linen or other fibre are woven into cloth.

loot

Stolen goods.

missionary

A person who sets out to change people's religious beliefs, especially by converting them to Christianity.

monastery

A building where a community of monks, and sometimes also nuns, lives, works and worships.

myth

A tale about gods or other superhuman creatures. Ancient myths often set out to explain how the world began, why dramatic natural events (e.g. earthquakes) happen, and why people behave as they do.

navigation

The skill of finding routes from place to place and of guiding ships safely along these routes.

noble

A man belonging to the high class of Vikings that was immediately below royalty but above freemen and slaves.

paganism

A system of religious belief that, unlike Judaism, Christianity and Islam, involves the worship of many gods.

parliament

A group of people that meets regularly to discuss political matters and make laws.

radioactive

(Of a substance) giving off energy in the form of particles or waves. By measuring the number of particles or waves given off, scientists can often work out how old the substance is.

raid

(verb) To attack and steal from.
(noun) A violent attack during which goods are usually stolen.

Roman alphabet

The alphabet that the Romans developed to write Latin, and that is now used to write English and many other European languages.

ruin

A building or group of buildings that has fallen down or been destroyed.

rune

The symbols that Vikings used to write on hard surfaces such as stone.

sacrifice

(verb) To kill (an animal or person) and offer it to a god as part of a religious ritual.
(noun) The killing of a person or animal in this way.

saga

Any of the books written in medieval Iceland and Scandinavia that tell both mythical stories about gods and factual stories about historical events. Many of the stories are set in Viking times.

sledge

A simple, open vehicle that is designed to travel over snow and is drawn by animals such as reindeer. The main part sits on top of two narrow wooden strips called runners.

spindle

A stick with a slot in the top designed to prepare wool for weaving.

tapestry

A fabric made by weaving strands of coloured thread together, and often featuring a picture or pattern.

turf

Grass dug up from the ground with roots and earth attached.

FURTHER READING

Cultural Atlas of the Viking World, James Graham-Campbell (editor), Colleen Batey, Helen Clarke, R. I. Page, Neil S. Price (authors) (Andromeda Oxford Limited, 1994)

Vikings!, Magnus Magnusson (The Bodley Head Ltd/BBC Books, 1980, 1992)

Blood of the Vikings, Julian Richards (Hodder and Stoughton, 2001)

afterlife 10
Alfred the Great 24
Althing 12, 13, 14, 15, 38
Ambrosiani, Dr Björn 21, 22
Ansgar 38
archaeology, history of 7, 42
Ari Thorgilsson (Ari the Learned) 13
armour 27
Asgard 37
'a-viking' 5, 11

Biddle, Berthe and Martin 25
Birka, Sweden 5, 15, 20–23, 38, 42
bishops 15
Brattahlid 16–19
brooches 19, 23, 34

Christianity and Christians 6, 15, 25, 34, 36, 37, 38–39, 40, 41, 43
cloth and clothes 19
cofferdams 29
craftspeople and workshops 20, 21, 22, 23
crime and punishment 14, 15
Crumlin-Pedersen, Dr Ole 29

Danelaw 24, 25
death 8
Denmark 4, 6, 17, 24, 28, 29, 38, 39, 41, 42

Eddas 6, 36
England 6, 24, 25
Erik the Red 16, 17, 18
Eriksson, Leif 17, 32, 33, 38

farmers 4, 9, 11, 13, 16, 17, 18, 19, 20, 23, 34, 37
food 16, 18, 23
France 25
freemen 8, 12, 14
Fröjel Discovery Programme 43

games 18
genetics 7
Germany 37, 38, 41
gods and goddesses 6, 34, 36–37, 41

Gokstad ship 28, 29
Gotland 28, 34–36, 42, 43
Gotland picture stones 35, 36
government 12–15
grave goods 8, 9, 10, 11, 21, 39
Great Army 24, 25, 27
Greenland 16, 17, 18, 24, 31, 38
Gustafsson, Gabriel 8, 9

Harald Bluetooth 38, 39, 40
helmets 5
Herjolfsson, Bjarni 32
houses and homes 16, 18, 19, 22, 32, 33

Iceland 6, 12, 13, 14, 15, 16, 36, 38
Ingstad, Helge and Anne Stine 33

Jelling 39–41
Jørgensen, Lars 43

Karlsefni, Thorfinn 33
knorrs 5, 30,
Krogh, Dr Knud 39

L'Anse-aux-Meadows 32–33, 42
Law-Speaker 14, 15
Lindisfarne 6
longships 5, 30, 31
loom 19

merchants 13, 20, 21, 23
metal-working 22, 23, 33, 35
myths 6, 35, 36, 41

navigation skills 31
nobles 8, 9, 10, 42
Normans 25
North America 6, 32, 33, 42
Norway 4, 6, 7, 8, 9, 16, 28, 29, 38, 41

Oseberg ship 7, 8–11, 28, 35

paganism and pagans 6, 15, 25, 34, 36, 37, 38, 40

radiocarbon dating 33, 42

reconstructions 19
religion 15, 34–39, 43
Repton, Derbyshire 24–27, 42
Rollo 25
Roskilde Fjord 28–31
runes and rune stones 39, 40–41
Russia 6, 20, 32, 34

sacrifice 34
sagas 6, 14, 18, 32, 33, 41, 42
ship-building 5, 30–31
ship burials 8–9, 28,
ships 4, 8, 20, 22, 28–33, 34
slaves 8, 9, 10, 11, 20
soldiers 26
Stolpe, Hjalmar 21, 42
Sturluson, Snorri 6, 36
Sun compass 31
Sweden 4, 6, 20, 21, 22, 23, 27, 34, 35, 37, 38, 41

Things 12, 13, 14, 15
Thingvellir 12–13, 14
Thor 26, 37, 43
Tingwall 15
Tissø, Lake 42
trade 4, 5, 20–23, 28, 34, 43
tree-ring dating 8
Tynwald 15

Valhalla 36, 37
Vinland 32, 33

war 5, 18, 24,
warriors 5, 24, 26, 28, 30, 31
weapons 23, 26
weaving 19
women 11, 16, 19, 27